# I Am a Little Monk

Written by Mi-hwa Joo
Illustrated by Hwa-kyeong Gahng
Edited by Joy Cowley

big & SMALL

Sawadeekrap! My name is Urt.
Actually, it is my nickname.
It means tadpole.
Everyone calls me Urt.

 Sawadeekrap and sawadeeka mean hello in Thai. For a man, you add "krap" at the end of the greeting. For a woman, you add "ka" to the end.

3

Click! First, lock the door.
Now look for the shaving cream.
I've found the white cream
Dad uses when he shaves.
I put this on my face and rub it.
This is how Dad's face gets clean.

Bu-urt is the time a Thai man spends in the temple trying to live as a monk. When you do Bu-urt you shave your head as well as your eyebrows and you meditate in the temple every day. Meditation is to close your eyes, sit down and think.

The hairdresser teases me:
"Urt, you have already shaved one eyebrow.
How could you be a monk at your age?
You are so lively and quick-tempered."

I don't care. I will be like my uncle.
He came back from Bu-urt and said that
when he meditated each morning,
his heart became relaxed.
I will do that too.

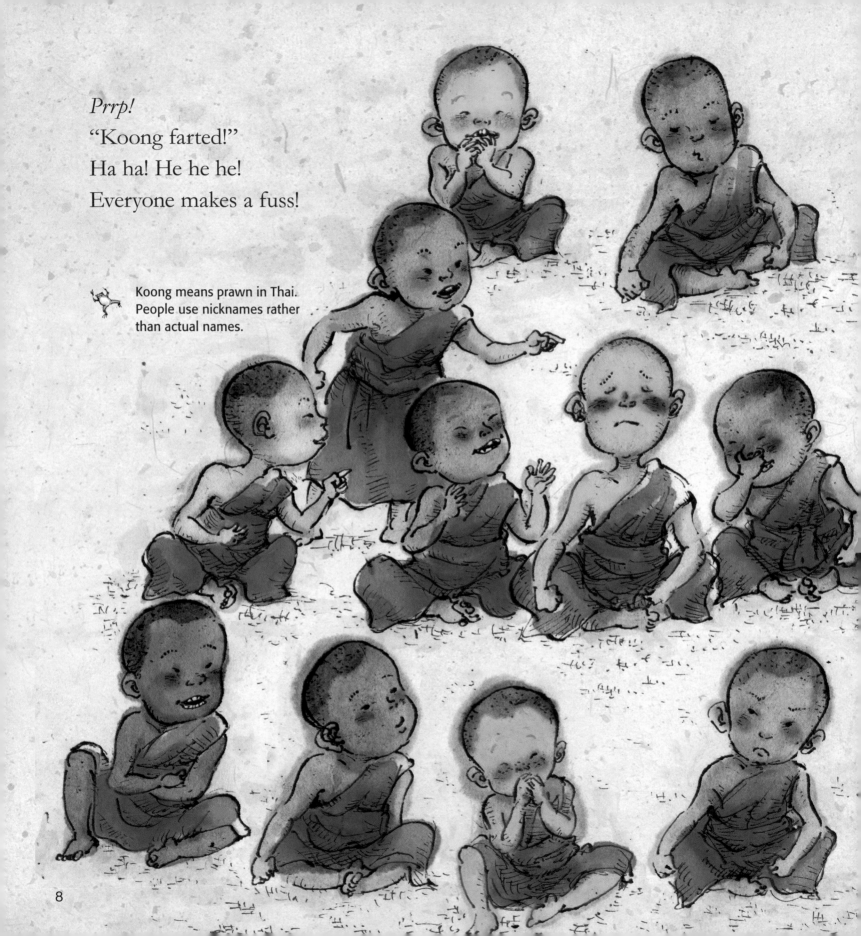

*Prrp!*

"Koong farted!"

Ha ha! He he he!

Everyone makes a fuss!

Koong means prawn in Thai.
People use nicknames rather
than actual names.

8

"Ahem!"
The big monk clears his throat
to restore order,
but we can't help laughing.

9

After the meditation time,
I have to clean the yard.
*Swipe swipe* goes the broom.
The monk told me to have a clean heart
just like the cleaning of the yard.
How can I clean my heart with a broom?

It is six in the morning, time to get food.

We go to town in groups.

Yesterday I went with the older brothers.

Today I am going on a boat with the big monk.

I like it better with the older brothers.

In Thailand, no matter how young you are, if you are doing Bu-urt, people will formally greet you as they would greet all monks.

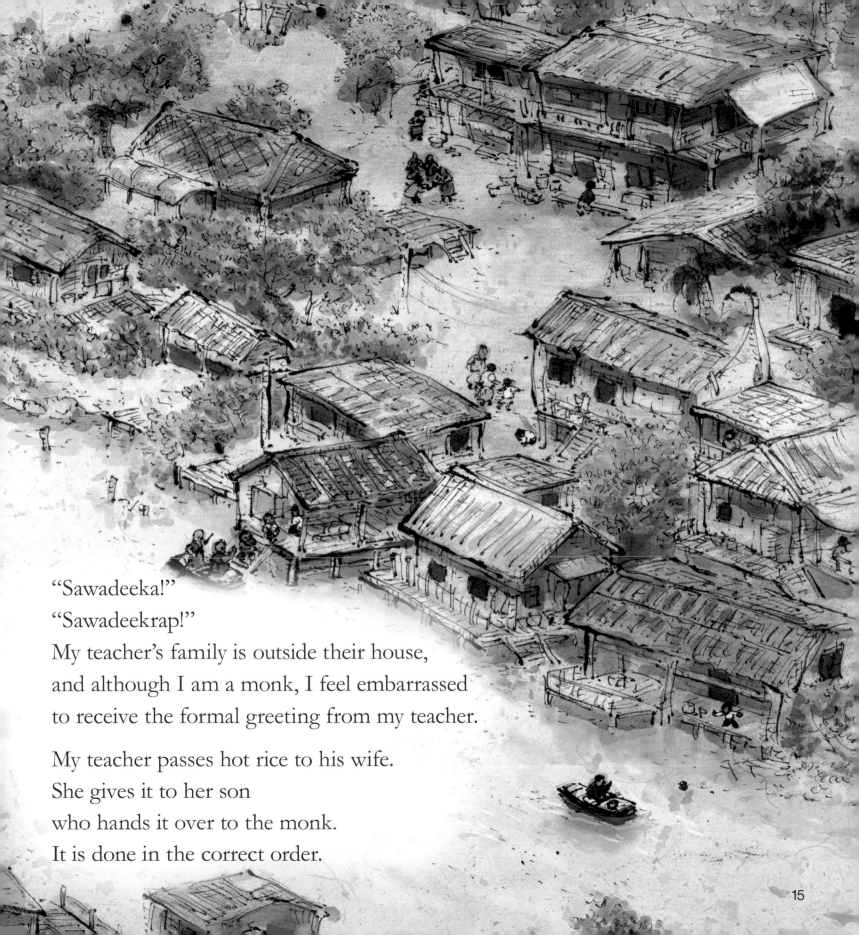

"Sawadeeka!"

"Sawadeekrap!"

My teacher's family is outside their house,
and although I am a monk, I feel embarrassed
to receive the formal greeting from my teacher.

My teacher passes hot rice to his wife.
She gives it to her son
who hands it over to the monk.
It is done in the correct order.

*Woof! Woof!*
I see a dog barking at foreign people.
That dog always barks at tourists.
I say, *"Tsk, tsk, tsk,"* to the dog
and I touch it on the tongue.
The dog backs off.

The monk said, "We must help others
whenever we can." That is why
I am helping the foreign tourists.

At last it is mealtime.
We're having sweet and sour
banana Som-Tam.
I am hungry. Shall I heap my plate?
No, I cannot be greedy
because we must share the food
we got from other people.

 Som-Tam is a salad made from papayas.
You can also make the salad with banana and cucumber.

Right now, my sister will be eating durian.

My friend will be drinking sweet coconut juice.

Although I ate, my stomach feels empty.

I remember the creamy caramel dessert

that Mom used to give me.

Mom, I miss you!

"Prince of fruits" is the nickname for durian. Although it is sweet and tasty,
the fruit has a nasty smell and cannot be taken on planes.
The Thais enjoy eating sweet things like durians after a meal.

Finally I am home.
I am not going to be greedy anymore.
I'm not going to fight with my sister.
I'm going to be nice.
I have learned a lot
by being a little monk.

It has been one week since I came home,

but it feels like a long time since I did Bu-urt.

I will never forget those times.

I am still called by my nickname

but I am more mature now.

I am not a naughty tadpole.

I am a respectable frog.

*Ggob! Ggob! Ggob!*

 Thai people say "ggob, ggob, ggob"
when they imitate the sound of frogs.

## About Thailand

# The Country of Buddhism and Monarchy

The flag of Thailand has horizontal stripes in red, white and blue. Red represents the people, white stands for Buddhism and blue is for the monarchy. This flag has been used since 1917. Before 1917, the national flag was plain red with a white elephant in the center. Thailand, the nation of Buddhism and monarchy, regards white elephants with great respect.

## Greet People with Your Hands Together

This Thai greeting is called "wai."

In Thailand, people greet each other with their hands pressed together. This greeting is called "wai." If you meet a friend or a younger person, you greet them by placing your hands together in front of your chest and bowing. If you meet a person a bit older, you place your two hands together on your chin and bow. If you meet a teacher, you greet them by placing your thumbs on your nose and bowing. If you meet a monk or a monarch, you greet them by placing your thumbs between your eyebrows before you bow.

## Calling People by Fun Nicknames

Even though Urt has a real name, his parents, teachers and friends call him by his nickname. Thai people often know others by their nicknames instead of their names. People do not get angry when they are called names like "Ggob" (frog) or "Koong" (prawn) or "Kai" (chicken) because this is part of Thai culture.

In Thailand, people often call each other by nicknames.

## Let's Try Being a Monk

Nine out of ten people in Thailand believe in Buddhism. A man from a Buddhist family goes into the temple once or more in his lifetime to live as a monk. This is called Bu-urt. It can be as short as a few days or as long as a few years.

## Daily Life of a Little Monk

Every day, monks go into town in groups to ask for food. In Buddhism, this is an essential part of becoming a monk. Little monks doing Bu-urt also go out to ask for food. After they come back from receiving food, they share what they have been given, separating it into two meals. Later they spend the day meditating and studying.

When you meditate, sit down, close your eyes and place your hands together.

### Little Monk's Timetable

| | | |
|---|---|---|
| | 5.00am: | Wake up |
| | 5.00 – 6.00am: | Memorizing Buddhist scriptures, meditating, cleaning |
| | 6.00 – 7.00am: | Go out to ask for food |
| | 7.00 – 8.00am: | Breakfast then Buddhist service |
| | 8.00 – 11.00am: | Studying Buddhist scriptures |
| | 11.00 – Noon: | Eating lunch with everyone |
| | Noon – 4.00pm: | Studying |
| | 4.00 – 8.00pm: | Buddhist service and free time |
| | 8.00pm: | Bed time |

## Every Monday Is Filled with Yellow

Like Japan and England, Thailand is a monarchy. The monarchy is highly respected and loved by the Thai people. In the cinemas, before a movie starts, a song for the King is played. No one sits down until the song is finished. Every Monday the streets are bright with yellow because people wear yellow shirts to wish the King the best of health.

Thai people wearing yellow on a Monday

## The Temples of Buddhism

Wat Phra Kaew is a temple located in Bangkok, the capital city of Thailand. Wat Phra Kaew is also called the Emerald Temple because the Emerald Buddha is enshrined there. Thai royal Buddhist events are often held in this temple.

A high mountain in Chiang Mai in northern Thailand is home to the famous Wat Phra That Doi Suthep temple. According to legend, the temple was built there after a white elephant climbed to the mountain's peak.

The Wat Phra Kaew temple in Bangkok

## Interesting Festivals

April is the hottest month in Thailand. Between the 13th and 15th of April, a large festival called Songkran takes place. The theme is water, and everybody floods the streets, shooting water pistols.

During November, north-eastern Thailand celebrates the Surin Elephant Round-Up Festival. A procession of up to 300 elephants makes its way through the streets accompanied by dancers and musicians in traditional costumes. This is followed by an event in a stadium where elephants and their handlers show off their skills with a series of games and performances.

Elsewhere during the year there are festivals for flowers, umbrellas, lanterns and many more interesting things.

During the Songkran festival, people have water fights.

# A Conversation with Surachat, Who Lives in Thailand

### Please introduce yourself.

Hello. I'm Surachat Chimroti and I live on the eastern side of Thailand in a place called Surin. I am ten years old.

### What do you like?

I like soccer. My favorite foods are chicken and the prince of fruits durian. Durian is really sweet and delicious.

### Have you done Bu-urt?

Yes, I did Bu-urt in April 2013. Before I did Bu-urt, I used to get scolded for being irresponsible and stubborn. However I changed a little bit after living in the temple. Now people say I have become more mature.

### What is your dream?

My dream is to become a pilot.

Indian Ocean

# Thailand

Name: Thailand

Location: Center of the Indochina peninsula in Southeast Asia

Area: 198,000 mi² (513,000 km²)

Capital: Bangkok

Population: Approx. 68,000,000 (2014)

Language: Thai

Religion: Buddhism

Main exports: Electrical appliances, computer parts, cars, rice

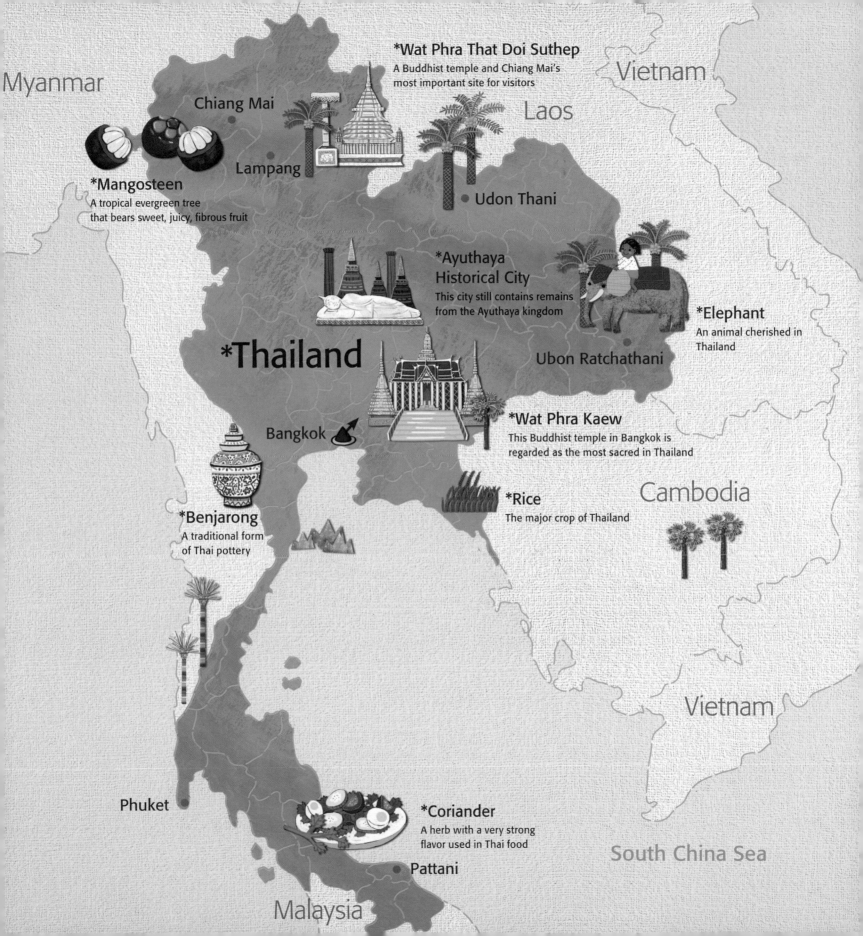

Myanmar

Vietnam

Laos

Chiang Mai

**\*Wat Phra That Doi Suthep**
A Buddhist temple and Chiang Mai's
most important site for visitors

Lampang

**\*Mangosteen**
A tropical evergreen tree
that bears sweet, juicy, fibrous fruit

Udon Thani

**\*Ayuthaya
Historical City**
This city still contains remains
from the Ayuthaya kingdom

**\*Elephant**
An animal cherished in
Thailand

**\*Thailand**

Ubon Ratchathani

Bangkok

**\*Wat Phra Kaew**
This Buddhist temple in Bangkok is
regarded as the most sacred in Thailand

Cambodia

**\*Benjarong**
A traditional form
of Thai pottery

**\*Rice**
The major crop of Thailand

Vietnam

Phuket

**\*Coriander**
A herb with a very strong
flavor used in Thai food

South China Sea

Pattani

Malaysia

Original Korean text by Mi-hwa Joo
Illustrations by Hwa-kyeong Gahng
Korean edition © Aram Publishing

This English edition published by big & SMALL in 2015
by arrangement with Aram Publishing
English text edited by Joy Cowley
English edition © big & SMALL 2015

Photo attributions by page no. - left to right, top to bottom
Pages 26: © Tevaprapas (CC-BY-3.0); public domain;
Page 27: all photos public domain; Page 28: © moaksey (CC-BY-2.0);
© unknown (CC-BY-2.0); © Takeaway (CC-BY-SA-3.0);
Page 29: public domain; public domain

ISBN: 978-1-925233-47-6

Printed in USA